EARLY THEMES

Sun, Moon, and Stars

by Frank Murphy,
Deborah Rovin-Murphy,
and Mary Beth Spann

SCHOLASTIC
PROFESSIONAL BOOKS

NEW YORK • TORONTO • LONDON • AUCKLAND • SYDNEY
MEXICO CITY • NEW DELHI • HONG KONG • BUENOS AIRES

"How the Moon Came to Be in the Sky," adapted from MOON STORIES by William Wiesner (Seabury Press, 1973)
"How Stars Came to Be in the Sky," adapted from TALES FOR TELLING FROM AROUND THE WORLD
selected by Mary Medlicott (Kingfisher, 1992)
"How the Sun Came to Be in the Sky," adapted from NORTH AMERICAN LEGENDS
edited by Virginia Haviland (William Collins, 1979)
"Night Comes…" from A BUNCH OF POEMS AND VERSES by Beatrice Schenk de Regniers.
Copyright © 1977 by Beatrice Schenk de Regniers. Used by permission of Marian Reiner for the author.

Edited by Joan Novelli
Cover design by Kelli Thompson
Cover art by Jo Lynn Alcorn
Interior design by Solutions by Design, Inc.
Interior illustration by James Graham Hale
Poster design by Kathy Massaro
Poster illustration by Jane Conteh-Morgan

ISBN: 0-439-16234-3

Contents

About This Book

Children of all ages are fascinated by the sun, moon, and stars they see in the sky. We need only tip our faces upward to be filled with the same sense of timeless awe and wonder. By becoming sky-watchers, young children can return to a time when people lived, worked, worshipped, and traveled in accordance with the sun, moon, and stars, while they are simultaneously being catapulted into a future filled with the promise of space discoveries, experiments, and exploration.

This book, one in a series of Early Themes books, is designed to capitalize on the natural curiosity and interest young children have about the sky above. It is filled with dozens of concept-building activities, including stories, movement exercises, games, explorations, and observations. To help children learn about the solar system, the book includes classroom ideas for making books, creating science-based art projects, singing songs, conducting experiments, collecting and recording data, and just plain wondering about the wonder of it all.

WHY TEACH WITH THEMES?

A thematic approach to teaching works well with young children for many reasons, including:

- Themes make teaching and learning fun and interesting. You can integrate core curriculum requirements into those themes that most appeal to children.

- Themes help unify and organize information. By weaving a common thematic thread through many different skills, concepts, bits of knowledge, and experiences, you can tie these loose ends together and help young students make sense of their world.

- Teaching with themes lets children build on prior knowledge and experience. With the confidence they already have about a familiar topic, children will be excited about learning new information.

GETTING STARTED

Children share a fascination for the world around them, including the one that is home to the sun, moon, and stars above them. This built-in motivation makes this theme unit a natural. Here are some tips for starting out and staying strong:

- Talk with students to discover what they know and want to know about the sun, the moon, and the stars. Record their responses on a three-column KWL chart (What We Know, What We Want to Know, What We Learned), leaving space to record the things they learn along the way.

- Invite students, families, and colleagues to lend topic-related toys, models, books, games, and audiovisual resources. Display contributions at a Sun, Moon, and Stars learning center that you set up. (See right.)

◎ Contact a local college or university to invite a speaker to visit your classroom and tell more about the sun, moon, and stars. When requesting a speaker, be specific about your needs. That way, you'll most likely connect with a speaker who can appropriately gear a presentation to your class.

◎ Plan a field trip to your local planetarium. Or, have a representative from the planetarium visit your class.

◎ Bookmark in advance web sites that children can use to locate information and resources related to the sun, moon, and stars. See Resources (page 6) for suggestions. Keep in mind that web site addresses and content change over time.

◎ Reserve a bulletin board or some wall space to build a thematically-based interactive word wall. (See Blast Off! Word Wall, page 9.)

◎ Visit your local children's library to borrow children's fiction and nonfiction books on outer space. (Literature Connections throughout this book suggest some of the best books for supporting your theme unit on the sun, moon, and stars.)

SETTING UP A LEARNING CENTER

Set up an attractive outer space learning center children can visit independently, in pairs, or in small groups. Here's how:

◎ Tape three sheets of oaktag together to form a three-sided display board. (Or, purchase a ready-made three-sided cardboard display unit.) Glue several pocket folders to the backdrop.

◎ Paint the board with black tempera paint to make a night sky. Paint over the pocket folders, too.

◎ Let the paint dry, then dip a toothbrush in white or silver paint and splatter-paint "stars" on the night sky background. (Do this by holding the brush over the black surface and dragging a craft stick across the brush bristles. Specks of paint will splatter to create a sparkly night sky background.)

◎ From separate pieces of cardboard, cut out a crescent moon shape (approximately 10 to 12 inches), a round sun shape (approximately 10 to 12 inches across) and some five-sided stars (approximately 6 to 8 inches across). Use yellow paint for the moon, orange for the sun, and gray or silver for the stars. Add sparkle to each shape with glitter. Glue the shapes to the night sky backdrop.

◎ Use packing tape to attach the board to a desk or table. Let children work together to cut out and decorate display letters to spell "Sun, Moon, and Stars." Glue them to the top of the board.

◎ Stock the center with writing supplies (sparkly pens, star stickers, and celestial stationery will be fun additions), copies of the Sky Journal log (see page 11), theme-related books, and pictures. In addition, you may choose to rotate space-related toys and games through the center. Use the learning center pockets to hold reproducible activities.

RESOURCES

Children's Books

Do Stars Have Points? by Melvin and Gilda Berger (Scholastic, 1998)

National Audubon Society First Field Guide: Night Sky by Gary Mechler (Scholastic, 1999)

Scholastic First Encyclopedia: All About Space by Sue Becklake (Scholastic, 1999)

Voyages of Discovery: Exploring Space by Editions Gallimard Jeunesse (Scholastic, 1993)

For Teachers

Astronomy Adventures by National Wildlife Federation (McGraw Hill, 1997). Play night sky bingo, go mining on the moon, and more, with 29 activities that teach about the history of astronomy, objects in the solar system, space exploration, and more.

Fresh & Fun: December by Bob Krech (Scholastic, 2000). This collection of dazzling and delightful activities, including many by teachers from across the country, features a section on "Stars." You'll find a fun game to get students moving, a "starry" word wheel that teaches word families, art projects, a poetry lesson, and more—all just right for young children!

Web Sites

Ask Jeeves for Kids! (**www.askjeeves.com**): This easy-to-use site lets children ask questions about the sun, moon, and stars, then click on links that contain answers.

Space.com (**space.com**): Share some out-of-the-ordinary views of stars, including spiraling stars, star storms, and the death of a star.

The Space Educators' Handbook (**vesuvius.jsc.nasa.gov/er/seh/**): This site features more than 2,000 files with photo clips, lesson plans, and activities flagged by grade level.

StarChild (**starchild.gsfc.nasa.gov**): This site is billed as "A Learning Center for Young Astronomers." Astronomy activities include versions for students of both primary and intermediate reading levels. Lots of related outer space links to explore.

Views of the Solar System (**www.solarviews.com**): Easy-to-understand information about the solar system.

Launching the Theme

Announce a unit on outer space exploration, and your class will be eager to take off! The activities in this section invite children to share what they already know, including space facts and words. They will also create "Sky Journals" for recording questions, observations, responses, and information as they progress through the unit.

Sky Journals

Students make learning logs to record responses to activities and questions, facts they learn, drawings, and so on.

Materials

- ◎ Sky Journal reproducible page (see page 11)
- ◎ yarn or stapler

Teaching the Lesson

1. Give each child five copies of page 11. Have children cut on the lines as indicated to make two Sky Journal pages from each.

2. Tell children to punch holes along the left side and string with yarn to bind. (They may also use a stapler to bind the pages.)

3. Ask children what kinds of things they might record in their Sky Journals—for example, as they study the sun, they might draw pictures of things they like to do on a sunny day, facts they know about the sun, and responses to class activities.

4. To get children started in their Sky Journals, have them create a cover on the first page. They can write a title and the author's name, and draw an appropriate picture.

5. Throughout the unit, look for opportunities for students to make entries in their Sky Journals. Take time to meet with individual students, asking questions to encourage them to share—for example, "What is your favorite page in your Sky Journal so far? Why?" and "What different kinds of things are in your Sky Journal?"

Star Students

Children record what they know about the sun, moon, and stars on star shapes, keeping extras on hand to record new information throughout the unit.

Teaching the Lesson

1. Make several star templates. (You can enlarge the template on page 12.) Enlist children's help in tracing and cutting out lots of stars.

2. Ask children to share information they know about the sun, moon, and stars. Record facts on stars (one per star), along with students' names, and display on a bulletin board or sheet of chart paper.

3. Place extra stars in an envelope and attach to the display. Encourage children to add to the Star Students display throughout the unit as they learn new information about the sun, moon, and stars.

Blast Off! Word Wall

Create a universe of words in your classroom with this word wall display. Use the word wall throughout the unit to explore spelling patterns and word families, and when writing journal entries, class newsletters, stories, and more. Your students' vocabulary will grow right along with the words on the wall!

Materials

◎ tagboard

◎ sun, moon, star templates (see page 12)

◎ markers

◎ Velcro®

Teaching the Lesson

1 Invite students to use the templates to trace and cut out sun, moon, and star shapes. You might set these materials out at the learning center and invite students to participate in small groups.

2 Start the word wall by writing the words *sun*, *moon*, and *star* on the shapes and displaying them on the wall. Invite children to add words they know that are related to the unit. Add those to the word wall.

3 Continue adding to the word wall as children learn new vocabulary during the unit. Take time to revisit words regularly to reinforce language skills.

ACTIVITY Extension Use the word wall to play language skill-building guessing games. For example, describe the features and/or meaning of one "sun" word and have children guess the word. ("I'm thinking of a word that begins with /s/ and ends with /t/ and tells about the time when the sun seems to disappear at the end of the day.") (*sunset*)

Literature Connection *Scholastic First Encyclopedia: All About Space* by Sue Becklake (Scholastic, 1999) tells about the solar system—including, of course, the sun, moon, and stars. Its design works well for young readers. Words that may be difficult are written in bold. A glossary lists and defines these words and is a good resource for building a word wall display.

Learning Center Link

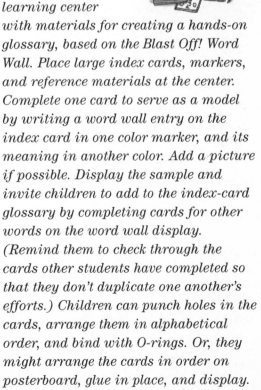

Stock your learning center with materials for creating a hands-on glossary, based on the Blast Off! Word Wall. Place large index cards, markers, and reference materials at the center. Complete one card to serve as a model by writing a word wall entry on the index card in one color marker, and its meaning in another color. Add a picture if possible. Display the sample and invite children to add to the index-card glossary by completing cards for other words on the word wall display. (Remind them to check through the cards other students have completed so that they don't duplicate one another's efforts.) Children can punch holes in the cards, arrange them in alphabetical order, and bind with O-rings. Or, they might arrange the cards in order on posterboard, glue in place, and display.

Teaching With the Poster:
"Night Comes..."

This poetry poster invites children to wonder about the night sky's stars and moon, and to think about the sun coming up, too—a perfect way to launch your theme unit. Revisit "Night Comes..." throughout the unit as children think of the sun, moon, and stars in new ways that enrich their appreciation of the poem.

Materials

◎ poetry poster (bound in center)

◎ drawing paper

◎ markers, crayons, paints, and other art supplies

◎ gel pens (optional)

Teaching the Lesson

1 Display the poster and read the poem aloud. Invite children to notice words that name actions, such as *leaking, peeking, sneaking, shaking,* and *quaking.*

2 Divide the class into groups and assign each an action word from the poem. Let children practice reading aloud their words, using voices and movements to interpret the author's meaning. Bring the class together to read aloud the poem again; this time students chime in on their group's words.

3 Invite children to tell why they think the author chose words like *leaking* and *peeking.* Ask what other words describe the way night comes—for example, do streets *light up*? Do neighborhoods *quiet down*? Do crickets *wake up*? What are some other changes they notice, especially about the sky?

4 Now ask children to imagine the sun coming up, first thing in the morning. What words tell what's happening in the sky? What other changes do children notice?

5 Give each child a sheet of drawing paper. Ask children to create a favorite early morning scene, using the illustration on the poster for inspiration, if they wish. (You might discuss ways to create a similarly gentle effect—for example, blending paint to soften edges.)

6 Have children use the poem as a model for "Day Comes..." poems. They can copy the poems on their pictures to create mini-posters. (Gel pens in contrasting colors work well for this.)

TIP: Give each child a copy of the poem to share at home. (See page 13.)

Name _____

SKY JOURNAL

Name _____

SKY JOURNAL

Sun, Moon, Star Templates

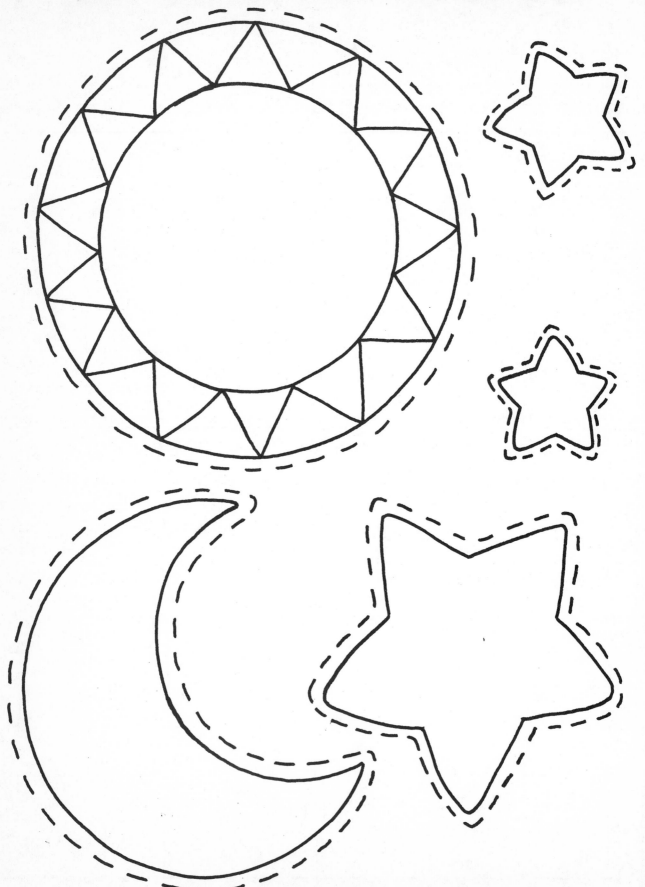

Early Themes: Sun, Moon & Stars Scholastic Professional Books

Night Comes...

Night comes
leaking
out of the sky.

Stars come
peeking.

Moon comes
sneaking,
silvery-sly.

Who is
shaking,
shivery-
quaking?

Who is afraid
of the night?

Not I.

—by Beatrice Schenk de Regniers

What do you see in the night sky?
Draw a picture to go with this poem.

From A BUNCH OF POEMS AND VERSES by Beatrice Schenk de Regniers. Copyright © 1977 by Beatrice Schenk de Regniers. Used by permission of Marian Reiner for the author. *Early Themes: Sun, Moon & Stars* Scholastic Professional Books

Sun

Celebrate the sun with the activities in this section, while exploring ways Earth's closest star gives us light, heat, and shade. Your students will meet a trickster hero in an ancient Native American myth, perform a mini-play, explore light and shadow, make a mini-book about sun safety, and more.

SCIENCE NOTES

The sun is an enormous ball of hot gases. Though positioned a full 93 million miles away from Earth, the sun still warms and lights our planet. Without the sun, life on Earth would not be possible. The sun is large compared to Earth—in fact, more than one million planets Earth could fit inside the sun! There are many stars that are bigger than the sun. The sun seems so big to us because it is closer than other stars. Other stars are so far away they seem like little dots of light in the sky. Stars, like the sun, can live for billions of years. Experts believe the sun is about 5 billion years old, and will burn for another 5 billion years before burning itself out.

Read Aloud Sun Lore:

How the Sun Came to Be in the Sky

Throughout history, people have worshipped the sun, and stories abound about the sun and how and why it hangs in the sky. Here is an ancient Native American sun story to share. In it, your students will meet Saynday, a trickster hero of the Kiowa Indians.

Materials

◎ How the Sun Came to Be in the Sky (see page 22)

Teaching the Lesson

1 How did the sun come to be in the sky? Ask children to listen closely for one answer as you read aloud the story.

2 After sharing the story, invite children to take turns retelling the story in their own words from beginning to end. Let one student begin, then other students add on to the story in turn. Write down their retelling on sentence strips for use in a later activity. (See Learning Center Link, right.)

3 Ask children why they think this story was first told. Explain that long ago, people told stories to explain events in nature and natural phenomena.

4 Just where in the sky is the sun? Use the Internet and other resources to locate a picture. (See page 6 for suggested web sites.) Have children identify the sun and the Earth. Ask: *How far away do you think the sun is from Earth?* (93 million miles) Though children will have difficulty grasping the magnitude of millions of miles, they'll have fun thinking about the answer when they see the sun in the sky.

TIP: Remind children not to look directly at the sun as this may cause damage to their eyes.

ACTIVITY Extension Team up children to create their own stories about how the sun came to be in the sky. Their stories may be serious or fanciful. Allow time for children to share their stories. You might audiotape them so that students can listen again on their own at the learning center.

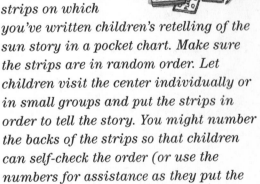

Learning Center Link

Place the sentence strips on which you've written children's retelling of the sun story in a pocket chart. Make sure the strips are in random order. Let children visit the center individually or in small groups and put the strips in order to tell the story. You might number the backs of the strips so that children can self-check the order (or use the numbers for assistance as they put the strips in order).

Literature Connection Share additional books and stories of sun myths from cultures around the world. Here's one to try: *Rupa Raises the Sun* by Marsha Wilson Chall (DK Publishing, 1998). Can your students guess what the main character's job is in this story? It's to hold the sun up in the sky!

Planet Lineup Mini-Play

This mini-play invites children to investigate the movement of the planets around the sun and learn about ordinal numbers at the same time.

Materials

- Planet-Lineup mini-play (see page 23)
- oaktag or manila file folders
- craft sticks

TIP: Add some flair to your students' mini-play production with an instrumental musical selection suggesting an interplanetary theme—for example, the sound track from *Star Wars* or *2001: A Space Odyssey*.

Teaching the Lesson

1. Make copies of the mini-play on page 23. Give each child a copy, then divide the class into groups of ten (one child for each part in the play).

2. Review the characters in the play, including the sun and the name of each planet.

3. Have children in each group make a prop for their character—for example, cutting out tagboard planets, decorating them accordingly, and gluing them to craft stick handles. Have picture resources on hand to help children prepare their props.

4. Discuss how children might position themselves as they perform the play.

The sun will be at the center of the planets. Planets can position themselves outward from the sun in order, with Mercury being the closest, followed by Venus, Earth, Mars, Jupiter, Saturn, Uranus, Neptune, and Pluto. Children can "orbit" the sun as they read their parts. (They may want to know that planets orbit the sun in a counterclockwise direction.)

5. Follow up children's performances by asking if anyone knows why the planets, including Earth, do not collide with one another or the sun. Though this is a difficult concept, guide children to understand that each planet has its own orbit—an invisible path that stays the same.

Literature Connection In the book *Postcards from Pluto* by Loreen Leedy (Holiday House, 1993), a group of students is given a guided tour of the solar system by a robot. After each stop, the young adventurers write postcards back home to share the information they have learned in a humorous but accurate way. After sharing the story, give each child a blank postcard to illustrate on one side and write a fact or two on the other. Send the postcards home to share with families.

ACTIVITY Extension Young children often believe that the sun moves across the sky. In reality, it is the Earth that is moving; the sun is stationary. Though this concept is too advanced for young children to understand, you can help lay a foundation for future understanding by guiding them to observe and talk about the sun's position in the sky and how it changes.

- Take children outside early on a sunny morning. Caution them not to look directly at the sun. Have children face north and hold their hands out to their sides. Ask: *Which hand points to the sun?*

- Repeat the activity at the end of the day, having students stand in the same spot (again facing north).

◎ Guide children to recognize that at the beginning of the day, their left hands point to the sun (east) and late in the afternoon, their right hands point to the sun (west). This is the sun "rising" and "setting," which is actually caused by the Earth rotating on its axis as it orbits the sun.

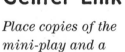 **Literature Connection** Help children better understand the science behind day and night by reading *Sun Up, Sun Down* by Gail Gibbons (Harcourt Brace, 1983).

Learning Center Link

Place copies of the mini-play and a set of props at the learning center. Invite children to perform the play on their own with classmates. They can take more than one part each to keep the groups small.

SCIENCE/DRAMATIC PLAY

Sun and Shadows

Plan some shadowy fun that will help children learn that some objects block the sun's light while others let sunlight through.

Materials

◎ objects with different degrees of opacity (black construction paper, clear plastic cups, tinted cellophane, craft sticks, pipe cleaners, etc.)

◎ Sun and Shadows record sheet (see page 24)

Teaching the Lesson

1 Divide the class into groups of three or four students each. Have each group gather a collection of objects from the classroom. Guide them in choosing objects with different degrees of opacity. (It's not necessary that children understand what this means—just suggest objects so that each group has some things that will block light and others that will let light pass through.)

2 Choose a sunny day to conduct your explorations. Take children outside, along with their collections of objects from the classroom and record sheets.

3 Invite children to notice shadows they see outside. Have them name the objects they think are making the shadows. Ask: *What do you notice about these objects?* Have children complete the first and second columns of their record sheets—listing the names of their objects and checking the appropriate space to show which they think will make shadows and which will not.

4 Let each group test the objects, setting them out in a clear space and noticing if they make shadows. Have them complete the record sheet to show their results.

Literature Connection Offer children a light source (such as flashlights) plus a copy of *The Little Book of Hand Shadows* by Phila H. Webb (Running Press, 1990) and encourage them to "try their hands" at hand-shadow play.

Learning Center Link

Provide materials to create shadow puppets to act out favorite stories. Have children draw and cut out animals, other characters, objects, even scenery from construction paper and tape them to craft sticks or straws. Have them practice their puppet shows without a light source first. For a class performance, provide an overhead projector as a light source for making shadows.

SCIENCE/ART

Watch Us Grow!

This activity helps children get a better picture of how Earth's movement relative to the sun changes the size and shape of shadows. They'll measure inches and feet and tell time to understand their results.

Materials

◎ Watch Us Grow! record sheets (see page 25)

◎ chalk

◎ measuring tapes

◎ clock or watch

◎ paper

◎ pencils

Teaching the Lesson

1. Take children outside early in the morning on a sunny day. Pair them up and give each team a piece of chalk, and each child a record sheet.

2. Find a safe area of pavement and have children trace one another's shadows. Pass around the measuring tapes and let children measure the length of their shadows. Have children record the time of day, and the length and description of their shadow on the record sheet. Ask them to draw a picture that shows their shadow and the position of the sun in the sky. (Remind them not to look directly at the sun.)

3. Repeat this activity several times over the course of the day, discussing the time, size of shadows, and position of the sun each time. Ask: *Is your shadow longer or shorter this time?* Guide children to notice that as the sun appears lower in the sky, their shadows lengthen.

ACTIVITY Extension Notice how the shadows of other objects change during the day. For example, if there is a tree visible from a classroom window, let children observe it several times during the day and record observations in pictures and words, as well as the time they made each observation.

Literature Connection *Bear Shadow* by Frank Asch (Aladdin, 1988) is a story about Little Bear's shadow. It gets in the way of his catching a fish, so he decides to get rid of it. No matter what Little Bear does, though, it won't go away. A cute story that shows how shadows are almost always with us when the sun is shining. Discuss and remind students how our shadows change size and position as the sun's position in the sky changes.

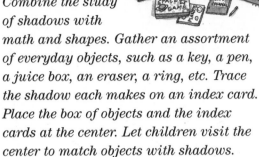
SCIENCE/ART

Sun Power

This activity introduces children to the power of the sun by helping them notice that sunlight has the ability to fade some materials.

Materials

- ◎ chair
- ◎ bright light source (such as an overhead projector)
- ◎ gray and black construction paper
- ◎ pencils
- ◎ scissors
- ◎ tape

Teaching the Lesson

1. Seat children, one at a time, in a chair positioned sideways against a wall backdrop so that the light source casts a shadow of the child's profile on the wall.

2. Have children take turns taping a piece of gray construction paper on the shadow and tracing around the seated child's silhouetted head shadow.

3. Let each child cut out his or her silhouette and tape it (from underneath) to a sheet of black construction paper.

4. Display in an area that receives a great deal of bright sunlight, such as a windowsill. When the paper on the outside has faded, have children remove their profile. Discuss reasons for the changes they see. (*Light from the sun causes the dyes in the paper to break down and fade.*) Ask: *Why didn't the area under your profiles fade?* (It was protected by the paper covering it.)

TIP: You can also use sun-sensitive photographic paper for this activity, which will produce faster results with more contrast. Paper is available through Educational Insights; (800) 933-3277. Also check local teacher-supply stores and science stores.

ACTIVITY Extension Have children use white copy paper to record questions they have about the sun. Cut out each child's question in a "word bubble" and display it near the corresponding silhouette. Title the display "What Sun Question Is on Your Mind?" Use the questions to guide mini-research projects and additional lessons.

Literature Connection Share books about the sun, such as *The Sun* by Seymour Simon (William Morrow, 1986). Invite children to look for "sun" words they can add to their Blast Off! Word Wall. (See page 9.)

Learning Center Link

Fill a shoebox or basket with a collection of objects, such as keys, leaves, small toys, coins, and so on. Provide dark-colored construction paper and tape. Invite children to make collages on the paper with the objects. (They can keep them in place by rolling pieces of tape to make it sticky on both sides.) Have children place their collages on a windowsill for a few days. They can check to see what's happening by peeking under one of the objects. When the paper around the objects has faded, have children remove the objects and display their silhouette art.

SCIENCE/MATH

T-Shirt Test

Ben Franklin didn't enjoy wearing the dark, heavy clothing that was common during Colonial times. He wanted to be more comfortable. So he performed an experiment to prove that light-colored clothing would be better worn in summer and dark-colored clothing better worn in winter. Let students try a similar experiment to learn more about the sun's power to provide warmth.

Materials

◎ two cotton T-shirts (one white, one black)

Teaching the Lesson

1. Lay two T-shirts side by side in hot sunlight for at least one hour.

2. Give each child a T-shirt graph marker. (See right.) Ask: *Which T-shirt do you think will absorb the most heat after one*

hour? Have children color their graph markers black or leave them white to show their prediction. Have children write their names on the cards, then place their cards on a class prediction graph.

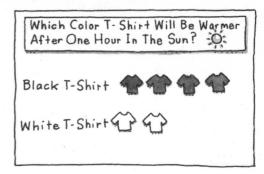

3. Have children take turns touching the two T-shirts to check their hypotheses against the results. Ask children to tell which colors (light or dark) they usually wear on hot, sunny days. Ask them which colors they might wear now, and why.

ACTIVITY Extension Try another version of this activity with a swatch cut from both a black and a white plastic trash bag and snow or crushed ice. Place each piece of plastic in a sunny spot on top of snow or crushed ice. Weigh down the plastic with pennies or small rocks in each corner. Check the snow under each piece of plastic every 30 minutes or so. What happens? (*The snow under the black plastic will melt.*)

SCIENCE/HEALTH

Safety in the Sun

Children "fill" a beach bag with pictures of things that help them stay safe in the sun.

Materials

- Safety in the Sun activity sheet (see page 26)
- scissors
- markers, crayons

TIP: In preparation for this activity, you might want to fill a real beach bag with sun-safety items, including sunglasses, sunscreen, water, an umbrella, a shirt, and a hat. Pull them out one at a time as you discuss how each helps people stay safe in the sun.

Teaching the Lesson

1. Give each child a copy of page 26. Let them color the beach bag and cut it out.

2. Invite children to name things that help them stay safe in the sun. Record their ideas on chart paper cut in the shape of a large beach bag.

3. Let children cut out pictures from magazines of sun-safety items and glue them on their beach bags.

4. Display beach bags and discuss the ways that each item keeps children safe in the sun.

ACTIVITY Extension Make a collaborative sun-safety class banner. Give each child a sheet of paper. Have children draw pictures of themselves doing a favorite sunny-day activity. Have them write or dictate sentences telling how they are playing safely in the sun. Tape pictures side to side to make a banner, and display.

Literature Connection *Sun Song* by Jean Marzollo (HarperCollins, 1995) uses lyrical rhyming text to describe Earth's movement in relation to the sun. The daily cycle of night and day is shown in a forest, on a farm, and with a young boy and his puppy.

How the Sun Came to Be in the Sky

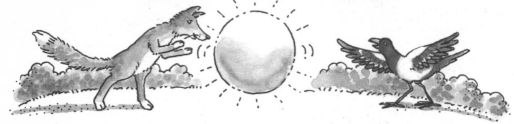

Long ago the world was different than it is today. On one side of the world, all the people and animals lived in darkness. On the other side there was sunlight. One day, an animal named Saynday was walking along, minding his way so as not to trip in the darkness. Oops, too late. He ran right into Fox, Magpie, and Deer, who were complaining about living in the darkness. They wanted the light, but the people and animals on the other side of the world refused to share. They agreed they would borrow the Sun from the people on the other side of the world. They would give the Sun back when they were through. They created a plan.

It was decided that Fox would travel to the other side of the world to see where the Sun was kept. When he arrived on the other side of the world, Fox found that the people there were playing with the Sun as though it were a ball. Fox made friends with the people, and they asked him to join the game. When it was his turn to roll the Sun, Fox picked up the Sun and began to run back to the dark side of the world. When Fox could run no more, Magpie met him on the road, and took the Sun and kept on running. When Magpie could run no more, Deer met her on the road, and took the Sun and kept on running.

"We have light now," said Saynday. But there was too much light. The Sun was too hot and too bright. The friends missed the darkness. They tried hiding the Sun in the teepee, but the light came through. They tried putting the Sun on top of the teepee, but the heat burned it down.

"Let's throw the Sun away," said Saynday. So they threw the Sun into the sky. There it stayed to give heat and light to both sides of the Earth—one side during the day and one side at night.

Adapted from *North American Legends* edited by Virginia Haviland (William Collins, 1979)
Early Themes: Sun, Moon & Stars Scholastic Professional Books

Planet Lineup Mini-Play

Characters: Sun, Mercury, Venus, Earth, Mars, Jupiter, Saturn, Uranus, Neptune, Pluto

Sun: I'm the Sun.
I give light and heat.
Don't you think that's really neat?
(Student raises Sun prop above his or her head.)

Mercury: I'm the first planet.
I'm next to the Sun.
So you can see, I'm the really hot one!
(Student walks in a circle closest to the Sun.)

Venus: I'm the second planet from the Sun.
That makes me so proud.
As you can see, I'm covered with clouds.
(Student walks around in second biggest circle.)

Earth: I am third.
I'm blue and green.
People live on me.
Try to keep me clean!
(Student walks around in third biggest circle.)

Mars: I am fourth from the Sun.
I'm very red.
Craters and volcanoes are on my head.
(Student walks around in fourth biggest circle.)

Jupiter: I'm fifth from the Sun.
I'm the biggest planet of the lot.
When you look at me, you'll see a big red spot.
(Student walks around in fifth biggest circle.)

Saturn: I'm sixth from the Sun,
With rings of rock and ice.
I have many moons. Isn't that nice?
(Student walks around in sixth biggest circle.)

Uranus: I'm seventh from the sun.
I always spin on my side!
Would you like to go for a ride?
(Student walks around in seventh biggest circle.)

Neptune: I'm eighth from the Sun.
I'm greenish blue.
I have a rocky center, too!
(Student walks around in eighth biggest circle.)

Pluto: I'm ninth in line.
The last from the Sun.
The smallest and coldest planet—I'm that one!
(Student walks around in biggest circle.)

Name _____

Date _____

Sun and Shadows

My Objects	My Prediction	My Results
	___ will make a shadow ___ will not make a shadow	___ makes a shadow ___ does not make a shadow
	___ will make a shadow ___ will not make a shadow	___ makes a shadow ___ does not make a shadow
	___ will make a shadow ___ will not make a shadow	___ makes a shadow ___ does not make a shadow
	___ will make a shadow ___ will not make a shadow	___ makes a shadow ___ does not make a shadow

Early Themes: Sun, Moon & Stars Scholastic Professional Books

Name _____ Date _____

Watch Us Grow!

Measuring My Shadow #1

Time _____

**Length of
My Shadow** _____

Picture of My Shadow
and the Sun in the Sky ➔

Measuring My Shadow #2

Time _____

**Length of
My Shadow** _____

Picture of My Shadow
and the Sun in the Sky ➔

Measuring My Shadow #3

Time _____

**Length of
My Shadow** _____

Picture of My Shadow
and the Sun in the Sky ➔

Early Themes: Sun, Moon & Stars Scholastic Professional Books

25

Name_____ Date _____

Safety in the Sun

Early Themes: Sun, Moon & Stars Scholastic Professional Books

Moon

Marvel at the moon with activities in this section that let your students explore what it feels like to walk on the moon, discover the phases of the moon, and learn how the moon shines. Your students will sing, experiment, play exciting games, and more.

SCIENCE NOTES

It takes the moon about 28 Earth days to spin on its axis and about 28 Earth days to make one trip around the Earth. When Earth spins on its axis, we experience day and night. When the moon rotates around the Earth, we experience moon phases (with less and less of the moon's surface visible to us as the month progresses).

The moon's surface is covered in dust and rocks. Large craters on the moon were created millions of years ago by falling chunks of rock and metal called *meteorites*. The moon has less gravity than the Earth, so people and spacecraft weigh less on the moon than on Earth.

Read Aloud Moon Myth:

How the Moon Came to Be in the Sky

Just as people from the beginning of time have wondered about the sun, they have wondered about the moon. People of all cultures have created stories about the moon and its reason for existing in the night sky. This activity begins with a read-aloud of a moon legend, versions of which have been told in India, Finland, and Czechoslovakia.

Materials

◎ How the Moon Came to Be in the Sky (see page 33)

◎ chart paper

Teaching the Lesson

1 Read aloud the moon story on page 33. Ask children to pay close attention to both the Moon's and Sun's actions in the story.

2 Following the story, set up a two-column chart. Label one side "Moon" and the other "Sun." Ask children to tell, in order, what happened to the Moon in the story. Have them do the same for the Sun. Compare the two characters using the chart students made. (*Both went to the party; the Moon nibbled on the cookies; the Sun ate lots and lots of cookies;* and so on.)

3 Have children think of other titles for the story—for example, because it also explains the sun's position in the sky, it could be called "How the Sun Came to Be in the Sky."

TIP: It might be fitting to share star-shaped cookies or crackers for children to nibble as you share the moon myth. Give children copies of the moon myth to share at home, too.

ACTIVITY Extension Make props to use in a dramatic retelling of the moon myth. Provide tagboard, scissors, and glitter. Have children use the materials to cut out sun, moon, and star shapes. Let them sprinkle glitter on the stars and attach the other shapes to craft sticks or straws. Children can take turns using the props to retell the story.

Literature Connection Use moon myths to introduce children to the waxing and waning of the moon. Try reading *The Birth of the Moon* by Coby Hol (North-South Books, 2000). Invite children to draw pictures of both a waxing and waning moon and to use words to explain the difference. (*A waning moon is decreasing in its visible surface. A waxing moon is increasing in its visible surface.*)

SCIENCE/LANGUAGE ARTS/MATH

Moon Phases Mini-Book

This project helps children learn to identify and label moon phases.

Materials

◎ Moon Phases mini-book (see pages 34–35)

◎ yellow and black crayons

◎ water, salt

◎ brushes

Teaching the Lesson

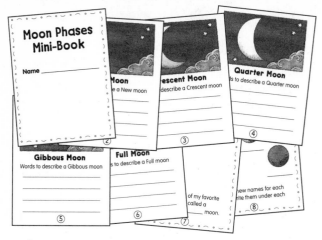

1. Give each child a copy of the Moon Phases mini-book pages. (Don't put the books together yet.)

2. Read pages 2 through 6 of the book together. Ask: *Do any of the moon phases you see look familiar?*

3. Have children use yellow crayons to color in the visible portion of each moon phase—the side we can see because it reflects the sun's light—and to use black crayons to color in the part of the moon that appears dark.

4. To create sparkling night sky pictures, have children lightly brush each page with water, then sprinkle salt on the paper while still wet.

5. When the pages are dry, have children sequence them, then staple together to bind.

6. Let children complete the last two pages in the book, drawing a picture of their favorite moon and labeling it on page 7, then making up new names for each moon on page 8. To go further, introduce some of the names Native Americans had for the moon each month. For example, September is a "Harvest Moon," December is a "Cold Moon," and May is a "Flower Moon." A good source for this is *Twelve Moons of the Year* by Hal Borland (G.K. Hall, 1985), a collection of nature essays.

ACTIVITY Extension Give children copies of the Moon Calendar (see page 36) and invite them to draw the shape of the moon they see each night throughout the month. If bedtimes or other constraints limit their observations, they can find pictures of the phases in the weather section of the newspaper. If you have Internet access, students may also check the following web sites for information about the phases of the moon:

The U.S. Naval Observatory's Astronomical Applications Department (**aa.usno.navy.mil/AA/faq/docs/moon_phases.html**): This site features pictures of each phase of the moon.

Virtual Reality Moon Phase Pictures (**tycho.usno.navy.mil/vphase.html**): This amazing site allows students to type in a month and year of their choice to see the phase of the moon for each day of that month. Students will have fun inputting the month and year they were born to see what the moon looked like in their first days.

Literature Connection Read *The Moon Seems to Change* by Franklyn M. Branley (HarperCollins, 1987). This book uses simple text with colorful diagrams to illustrate the phases of the moon.

TIP: Why does the moon seem to change shape? The answer to this question involves concepts that are too difficult for young children to grasp. For this reason, activities that model the sun reflecting light on the moon may be inappropriate. Sharing books such as *The Moon Seems to Change* and allowing children to experiment with simple models, such as the one described in the book, will help lay a foundation for future understanding.

Moon Spinner Movement Game

Children will enjoy learning about the phases of the moon with this active game.

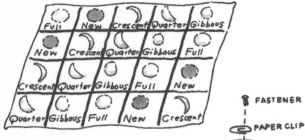

Materials

- ◎ flat, white twin bedsheet
- ◎ yardstick or meterstick
- ◎ fabric paints or fabric markers
- ◎ reproducible spinner (see page 37)
- ◎ oaktag
- ◎ scissors
- ◎ paper clip
- ◎ brass fastener
- ◎ rocks or books

Teaching the Lesson

1. Make a moon mat by dividing the sheet into 20 equal parts (5 across, 4 down). Use fabric paints or markers to draw and label one of the five moon phases in each section. Each moon phase should be represented four times on the mat.

2. Copy the spinner pattern and glue it to oaktag. Color with markers, if desired. Use scissors to punch a hole in the middle of the spinner. Place a paper clip over the hole, as shown. (See illustration, above.) Insert the brass fastener through the paper clip and hole. Spread the fastener tabs apart on the back of the spinner. Make certain the paper clip can spin freely.

3. Spread the moon mat on a grassy or carpeted surface. Use small rocks or books to hold the edges of the mat in place. Look together at the mat; have children read the mat and identify the different moon phases represented.

4. Show children the spinner. Explain that to play this game, they will take turns spinning the spinner and placing their hands and feet on the mat as directed by the spinner.

5. Begin playing with three children, letting each child spin and move in turn. Continue playing until one child loses his or her balance and tumbles down. Play again with a new group of players.

Literature Connection *Moon Man* by Tomi Ungerer (Roberts Rinehart, 1998) is a tale about how the man in the moon travels to Earth to join earthlings dancing and singing. When people become afraid of him, he is put in jail. Students will enjoy watching Moon Man escape from jail with the help of his changing phases!

Learning Center Link

Create a moon card game modeled after the card game "War." Place pictures of the different phases of the moon in a large envelope. Have students play with partners, taking turns pulling a moon card out of the envelope. The player whose card displays a fuller moon wins the two cards. When finished, players can put the cards back in the envelope and play again.

Moon Tunes "Piggyback" Song

Teaching the Lesson

1 Print the lyrics to the following song on sentence strips and place them in a pocket chart.

What Is It Like on the Moon?
(Sing to the tune of "London Bridge Is Falling Down")

What is it like on the moon?
On the moon? On the moon?
There is no sound on the moon.
It is quiet.

What is it like on the moon?
On the moon? On the moon?
There is little gravity on the moon.
You can bounce.

What is it like on the moon?
On the moon? On the moon?
You need a spacesuit on the moon.
There is no air.

What is it like on the moon?
On the moon? On the moon?
There are craters on the moon.
Watch your step!

2 Before singing the song, tap children's prior knowledge. Do they know what it is like on the moon? What do the astronauts on the moon wear? Would they like to go to the moon?

3 Sing a verse of "London Bridge" to acquaint children with the tune, then follow the words in the pocket chart to sing about the moon. Create movements to go with each part of the song. (*There is no sound on the moon*—students put their fingers to their lips. *There is little gravity on the moon*—students pretend to bounce. *You need a spacesuit on the moon*—students pretend to put on a helmet. *There are craters on the moon*—students pretend to step or hop over a crater.)

4 Store pocket chart pieces in a manila envelope so students can put favorite phrases back into the song and act it out on their own or with a small group.

TIP: Make copies of the song for children to share at home. (See page 38.)

ACTIVITY Extension Invite students to feel what it is like to walk on the moon. Use large rubber bands to attach two large sponges to a child's feet. Let children take turns with the sponges, walking around the room to get a feeling for weightlessness.

Learning Center Link

Strengthen number recognition with crater math. Punch 10 holes (randomly) in a sturdy paper plate. Place a container of marbles and cards labeled 1-10 at the center. Have students choose a card and place that number of marbles in the craters on the moon.

Literature Connection Aspiring astronauts will enjoy *I Want to Be an Astronaut* by Byron Barton (HarperCollins 1998), an easy-to-read book with simple pictures that show what it is like to be an astronaut.

Does the Moon Shine?

This simple activity can help children understand that even though the moon looks like it is shining at night, it is not a luminous body. The moon shines because it is reflecting the light from the sun.

Materials

◎ foil (cut into a circle)

◎ flashlight

◎ tape

Teaching the Lesson

1 Start with a survey. Ask students to raise their hands if they think the moon shines. Record results. Explain that the class will be doing an experiment to answer this question.

2 Take the foil circle and tape it to the chalkboard. Turn off the light and shine the flashlight onto the foil. What happens? (*The foil reflects the light of the flashlight and appears to shine in the dark room.*)

3 Turn off the light again, but this time do not shine the flashlight. What happens? (*The foil doesn't shine because it has no light source to reflect.*)

4 Explain to students that the moon appears to shine because it reflects the light of the sun.

Literature Connection Dav Pilkey's *The Moonglow Roll-O-Rama* (Orchard, 1995) is a fanciful rhyming story that answers the question, "Have you ever wondered where animals go, at night when the light of the moon is aglow?" Bright, bold, and dreamy illustrations complement the lyrical text.

ACTIVITY Extension Use Dav Pilkey's illustrations as a chance to introduce Van Gogh's famous painting, "Starry Night." Invite students to create their own night sky paintings. Give students a sheet of white construction paper and yellow crayons. Have students draw and color a moon and some stars with crayon. (Remind students to press firmly when coloring.) After stars and moon are completed, have students brush black watercolor paint over the paper—even covering their stars and moon! The waxy crayon drawing will shine through. For more effect, use purple and blue watercolor paint over the black paint.

How the Moon Came to Be in the Sky

At the beginning of time, North Wind invited his nephew, Sun, and niece, Moon, to a party. Sun and Moon's mother, the Sky, washed her two children's faces until they both shone. "Please behave at the party," she told them, "and don't be greedy!"

At the party, the North Wind served beautiful star-shaped cookies covered with glittery golden frosting. He told Sun and Moon to help themselves to as many as they wished. Moon nibbled on a few star cookies and placed the rest into her purse to take home to her mother. Sun, however, could not get enough of the star cookies—he ate and ate and ate until he was quite plump and flushed from eating so much.

When the children returned home, Moon opened her purse and shared the star cookies with her mother. "There are too many to eat!" exclaimed Sky Mother. "I shall decorate my cape with them." So she fastened the stars to her dark night cape where they sparkled and shone. Sky Mother was pleased; she gave Moon a cool and calm spot in her night sky so Moon could watch over the stars.

But Sky Mother was angry when she saw how red and hot Sun's face was from eating so much. "I can tell you were very greedy, Sun!" she cried. "You ate too much. You did not listen to me, and I am ashamed of you!"

Sun felt angry at Sky Mother's words. "I don't want to do what you say!" cried Sun. "I don't want to be near you! I want to go far away from you!" So Sun flew far away from the night sky. He found his own spot in the center of the Universe, where even today he shines plump and bright.

Adapted from *Moon Stories* by William Wiesner (Seabury Press, 1973)
Early Themes: Sun, Moon & Stars Scholastic Professional Books

Moon Phases Mini-Book

Name _____

New Moon

Words to describe a New moon

_____

_____

_____

_____

②

Crescent Moon

Words to describe a Crescent moon

_____

_____

_____

_____

③

Quarter Moon

Words to describe a Quarter moon

_____

_____

_____

_____

④

Early Themes: Sun, Moon & Stars Scholastic Professional Books

Gibbous Moon

Words to describe a Gibbous moon

_____

_____

_____

_____

⑤

Full Moon

Words to describe a Full moon

_____

_____

_____

_____

⑥

Here is a picture of my favorite moon phase. It is called a

_____ moon.

⑦

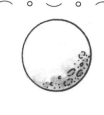

_____   _____

Make up a new name for each moon phase.

⑧

_____'s Moon Calendar

For the Month of _____

MONDAY	TUESDAY	WEDNESDAY	THURSDAY	FRIDAY

New

Crescent

Quarter

Gibbous

Full

Early Themes: Sun, Moon & Stars Scholastic Professional Books

Moon Spinner

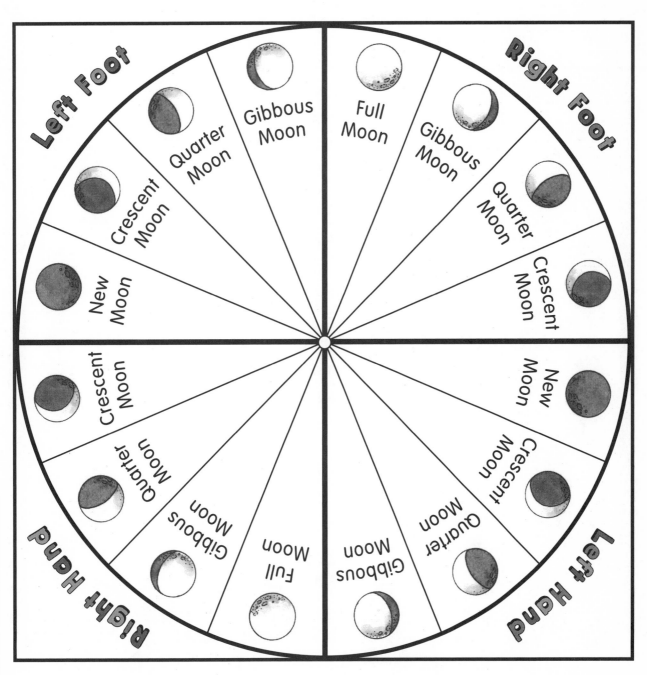

Early Themes: Sun, Moon & Stars Scholastic Professional Books

What Is It Like on the Moon?

(Sing to the tune of "London Bridge Is Falling Down")

What is it like on the moon?
On the moon? On the moon?
There is no sound on the moon.
It is quiet.

What is it like on the moon?
On the moon? On the moon?
There is little gravity on the moon.
You can float.

What is it like on the moon?
On the moon? On the moon?
You need a spacesuit on the moon.
There is no air.

What is it like on the moon?
On the moon? On the moon?
There are craters on the moon.
Watch your step!

Early Themes: Sun, Moon & Stars Scholastic Professional Books

Stars

Twinkle! Twinkle! Since time began, the starry "diamonds in the sky" have inspired everything from artwork to wishes. This section includes a Chinese-inspired star story to share, and offers children activities that will look at how stars twinkle, the color and age of stars, the constellations, and more.

SCIENCE NOTES

Stars begin as clouds of dust and hydrogen gas. When the gas and dust are drawn together, they clump up, become hotter and hotter, and form stars. A star cloud is actually called a *nebula*—the term the Romans used for *cloud*. It takes about 50 million years for a star to become so hot in the center that it shines. People use the North Star as a guiding star because it hardly moves in the sky.

Twinkle, Twinkle

Children begin their investigation of the stars with a science experiment that shows why stars twinkle.

Materials

◎ overhead projector
◎ bowl filled halfway with water
◎ paper

Teaching the Lesson

1. Place the bowl with water on the overhead projector.

2. Cut a hole (a couple of inches across is sufficient) from the middle of a sheet of paper. Place the paper over the bowl, centering the hole in the middle.

3. Turn off the lights and turn on the projector. Tap the bowl so that the water moves gently.

4. Students will observe that the light projected by the hole in the paper seems to twinkle. Explain that we look at stars through Earth's air, which is always moving. Movement blurs starlight as it travels to Earth, making stars appear to twinkle. The movement of the water bent the light rays so that the light on the wall appeared to twinkle.

ACTIVITY Extension Use the song "Twinkle, Twinkle, Little Star" as a springboard for teaching rhyming words. Write the song on sentence strips. Place in a pocket chart. Ask students to find the words in the poem that rhyme. Write these words on star shapes and place them in the pocket chart. Let children write new rhyming words on star shapes and add them to the pocket chart, placing them alongside the words from the poem that rhyme.

Learning Center Link

Place the rhyming word stars at a center. Make a sparkly paper-towel tube telescope. (Cover the tube with blue construction paper and sprinkle with gold glitter.) Invite children to spread out the stars on the table or floor and use the telescope to search for rhyming pairs.

Literature Connection *Why Do Stars Twinkle?* by Isaac Asimov (Gareth Stevens, 1991) is above-level for K-1 students, but offers colorful photos, illustrations, and diagrams with explanations about why stars twinkle. Share information in the book by reading portions aloud—for example, how a hot pavement in the summertime seems to shimmer. (Though this book is currently out of print, you may find a copy in your library or through Amazon.com or other Internet services.)

Collaborative Constellations

Students get to feel like part of the universe by creating a collaborative constellation.

Materials

- ◎ laminated construction paper stars
- ◎ small flashlights (enough for several groups)
- ◎ Constellation Cards (see page 44)

Teaching the Lesson

1. Begin by taping down a few construction paper stars on the floor to form one of the more common constellations, such as the Big Dipper.

2. Choose students to stand on the stars. Give each child on a star a flashlight. Have students shine their flashlights straight up toward the ceiling, then turn off the room lights to see a constellation on the ceiling.

3. Have students work in small groups to make more constellations. Give everyone a "ready" signal before turning off the lights, then darken the room and watch the starry sky light up.

ACTIVITY Extension Supply students with laminated stars. Have them form small groups and create their own constellations. Stage a constellation presentation where each group presents their constellation to the class. Let the class guess what the constellation is supposed to be. (Display pictures of constellations for reference.)

Learning Center Link

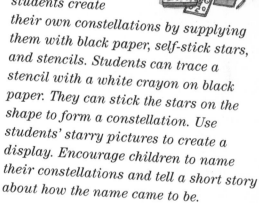

Have individual students create their own constellations by supplying them with black paper, self-stick stars, and stencils. Students can trace a stencil with a white crayon on black paper. They can stick the stars on the shape to form a constellation. Use students' starry pictures to create a display. Encourage children to name their constellations and tell a short story about how the name came to be.

Literature Connection Two literature selections just right for sharing simple information about stars are *I Am a Star* by Jean Marzollo (Scholastic, 2000) and *Stars* by Jennifer Dussling (Grosset & Dunlap, 1996). Both selections have interesting and colorful illustrations with easy-to-read text perfect for kindergarten and first grade.

How Old Is That Star?

In this activity students gain knowledge about the age of a star as well as practice math by lining up according to age.

Materials

◎ stars cut from red, yellow, and blue paper

Teaching the Lesson

1 Ask children how they can tell if a tree is young or old—for example, by noticing how tall the tree is, how wide its trunk is, and how many branches it has.

2 Tell children that scientists can tell how old stars are by looking at them through telescopes. Explain that the newest stars are blue, the oldest stars are red, and the middle-aged stars, like the sun, are yellow.

3 Have the class line up according to age. This is a good opportunity to use the calendar to see the order of the months. Children sharing the same month can also compare birth date numbers.

4 When students have lined up correctly, distribute red stars to the oldest students, yellow stars to the students in the middle, and blue stars to the youngest students. Go further by asking all of the "oldest stars" to step forward, followed by the middle stars, and the youngest stars.

ACTIVITY Extension Have students group themselves by star color. Then have them compare month and date to arrange themselves in age-order. Follow up by having students create a class graph comparing the number of children born in each month.

Literature Connection *Stars* by Seymour Simon (William Morrow, 1986) features wonderful photographs of different types of stars. It also offers information about the temperatures of new and old stars.

Read Aloud Star Story:
How Stars Came to Be in the Sky

Long ago people made up fantastic stories to explain how things occurred in nature. This activity begins with a Chinese story of how the stars came to be in the sky.

Materials

◎ How Stars Came to Be in the Sky (see page 45)

Teaching the Lesson

1 How did the stars come to be in the sky? Ask children to listen closely for

the answer as you read aloud the story on page 45.

2 After sharing the story, invite children to take turns retelling the story in their own words from beginning to end. Let one student begin, then other students add on to the story in turn. Write down their retelling on sentence strips for use in a later activity. (See Learning Center Link, page 15.)

3 Ask children why they think this story was first told. Explain that long ago, people told stories to explain events in nature and natural phenomena.

4 Have students share their own fanciful ideas about how the stars came to be in the sky.

ACTIVITY Extension Use a hole punch to make holes in several sheets of black construction paper. Distribute a sheet of hole-punched black construction paper and some stick-on foil stars to pairs of students. Tell students that they need to mend their night sky. Students use their counting skills to match the number of "sky holes" in the paper to the number of foil pieces they will need. Students can then use the foil stars to "mend" the sky, sticking them over the holes. Go further by having children write a sentence that tells how many stars they used to mend the sky.

Literature Connection *Stargazers* by Gail Gibbons (Holiday House, 1992) includes information about stars, from how constellations were named to how telescopes work. Colorful illustrations with simple text and easy-to-read diagrams make this a perfect read aloud to answer basic stargazing questions.

Learning Center Link

Give children a little piece of the starry night sky by having them make their own telescope. Place paper towel tubes, black paper cut into circles (bigger than the opening of the tube), paper clips (opened up), and rubber bands at the center. Have students place a black paper circle on one end of a tube, and secure with a rubber band. Have them punch holes through the black paper with the end of a paper clip in any design they wish. When they are finished, they can hold the telescope up to the light and look through to see their own starry sky.

Constellation Cards

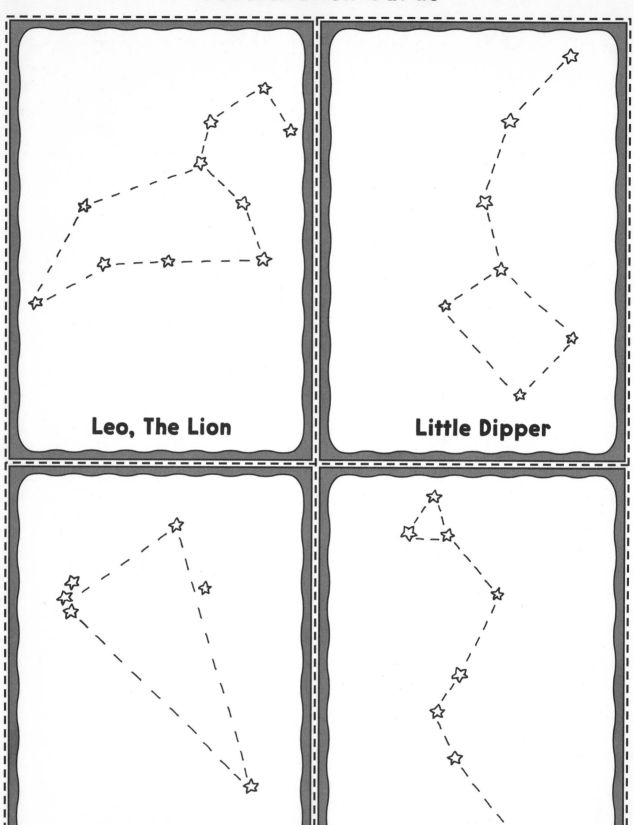

Leo, The Lion

Little Dipper

Triangulum,
The Triangle

Serpens, The Serpent

Early Themes: Sun, Moon & Stars Scholastic Professional Books

How Stars Came to Be in the Sky

Long ago when the world was new, some children were playing in the grass. SPLAT! Something fell right where they were playing. It was flat and blue. The children looked closer, but could not tell what it was. Suddenly, more blue things fell. SPLAT! SPLAT! SPLAT! The children looked up and realized the sky was falling down in pieces. Each time a piece fell, it left a hole in the sky. Blackness spread out from each hole, turning the blue sky black.

The children ran to tell the wise woman that the sky was falling. She told the children she would mend the sky holes. She told them to gather together all the pieces of the sky. The children looked everywhere and gathered all the pieces they could find. The wise woman counted all the holes and then she counted all the sky pieces. There were more holes than pieces.

"We can gather pretty colored stones and fill the sky holes with those," said the wise woman. But the children were sad. They wanted the sky to be as it was before: blue during the day and black at night. "All right," said the wise woman. "I will fix the sky holes so the daytime sky will look all blue. But you must let me work in secret."

So the wise woman built a ladder to the sky. Then she worked all night. The next morning the children were delighted because the entire sky was blue. During the day they couldn't see how the wise woman had mended the sky, but at night they saw a wonderful surprise: Into each hole, the wise woman had placed a shiny silver star. The children couldn't see the stars in the daylight, but when they went out at night, they saw a sky filled with twinkling stars. And on a clear night, you can see those same stars glittering through "sky holes," too!

Adapted from *Tales for Telling From Around the World* selected by Mary Medlicott (Kingfisher, 1992)
Early Themes: Sun, Moon & Stars Scholastic Professional Books

Celestial Celebration

Wrap up your Sun, Moon, and Stars unit with an out-of-this-world celebration that lets children share their learning with families and other guests. In doing so, children can revisit concepts and build on their understanding. Such a celebration also promotes children's pride in their work, and a sense of accomplishment in all they've learned.

Sun, Moon, and Stars Tablecloth

Visit a party store or variety store to purchase inexpensive plain blue paper tablecloths, or cut blue craft paper to fit your tables. Use sun, moon, and star templates (see page 12) to make stencils. (Trace the pattern on sturdy paper and cut it out, leaving a sun-, star-, or moon-shaped stencil in the paper.) Place the tablecloth(s) on the floor, and let children dip sponges in yellow tempera paint, blot until almost dry, then use to stencil suns, moons, and stars on the tablecloths. Sprinkle with glitter and let dry.

COOKING

Sun, Moon, and Star Snacks

Here are three treats children can help make for their Celestial Celebration.

Teaching the Lesson

1 Make moon cookies. Have children cut circular cookies from refrigerator sugar cookie dough. Have children use fingers to gently reshape cookies into crescents. Bake according to package directions. Frost, place on waxed paper, and sprinkle with yellow sugar crystals.

LANGUAGE ARTS

Celestial Celebration Invitation

Provide children with sun, moon, and star templates. (See page 12.) Let them use them to create one-of-a-kind invitations. For example, they might trace a crescent-moon shape on accordion-folded paper to make a fold-out invitation. Or, they might combine the shapes to make a collage invitation. Together, brainstorm information to include on the invitation. Write this on chart paper for students to copy on their invitations. As children return with information about who will be attending, use tallies to keep count.

2 Serve up some starry sandwiches. Have children use a star-shaped cookie cutter to cut bread into star shapes. Spread with cream cheese and jam, or layer with sandwich fillings and top with a second star-shaped piece of bread.

3 To make sun tea, place several non-caffeinated or herbal tea bags into a clear plastic container. Fill the container with water, cover, and place in the sun until brewed. Serve with lemon wedges.

TIP: Check for food allergies before letting children enjoy their sun, moon, and star snacks.

Literature Connection Read aloud the book *The Magic School Bus Lost in the Solar System* by Joanna Cole (Scholastic, 1990). Challenge children to dress as Ms. (or Mr.!) Frizzle for your Celestial Celebration. Children can use fabric markers to decorate white T-shirts with suns, moons, and stars, or they may cut out shapes and designs from construction paper and tape them to their regular clothes. Remind children to decorate their shoes à la Ms. Frizzle!

During the Celebration

The following are suggestions for incorporating some of the activities and ideas in this book into your celebration:

◎ Have small groups of children make constellations to share with guests by putting stars on the floor in the shape of the Big Dipper or other constellation and standing on them. Dim the lights and have your

"stars" shine flashlights on the ceiling. (See page 41.)

◎ Have students make shadow puppets and display using an overhead projector. (See Learning Center Link, page 18.)

◎ Perform the mini-play, Planet Lineup. (See page 23.)

◎ Sing a moon song. (See page 38).

◎ Invite children and their guests to find a quiet place to enjoy a theme-based book together. (See Literature Connections throughout.) Encourage children to share their moon mini-books with guests, too. (See page 28.)

◎ Let children and their guests read words from the Blast Off! Word Wall. (See page 9.)

◎ Let children practice and share the read-aloud stories about the sun, moon, and stars. (See pages 22, 33, and 45.)

◎ Separate the room into three distinct sections: Sun, Moon, and Stars. Display appropriate projects in each area.

TIP: Have students create space helmets out of grocery paper bags and art materials to use as they act as tour guides around the room.